Black & White Clouds of
Tearful Testimonies

Black & White Clouds of Tearful Testimonies

Black & White Clouds Testimonies

LaMark Junior Combs Sr.

To order additional copies of this book, contact:
Xlibris Corporation
1-888-795-4274
www.Xlibris.com
Orders@Xlibris.com
36654

Contents

Dedication

Bringing together the Pieces of the Conscious and Unconscious Lives

We are conscious and unconscious of many things that happen in a split second, as our lives. The timeless count down is approaching upon the temples, which embraces the souls. Come let us sit quietly at a round table that holds the cup of wisdom, knowledge, and understanding that will grow from a mustard seed of faith.

"With men this is impossible, but with God all things are possible."

Dedicated to those lost, but now found, as for my siblings in Christ Jesus.

BLACK & WHITE CLOUDS OF TEARFUL TESTIMONIES

Stand on the black clouds that allow you to witness the downpour of many testimonies. As we awake to sit quietly on the side of our beds that which we lie through many sleepless nights. No longer able to sit or shut out the outcries of many harmless shadows that are separated from the bodies that embrace their souls. We are now taking the stands as we lift our right hand to take the oath. Tell nothing but the truth so help us God is said as we repeat those words that ring in the ears of many. We have witnessed the good and the evil that possesses the minds and hearts that portray those images within our naked eyes. Our testimonies are to reach those who are unable to hear or see the prolonged disastrous storms of the past and future. The storm permits a downpour of allegations that could lead us to believe that justice has prevailed. The judgment of many is sought out by their tearful testimonies that create a puddle of truth. View the expectation of the good book that is recognized when presented to us without beginning or end.

A BEAT AWAY FROM

For I'm only an ambitious might that has to seek an influential being. It's a scale that only weighs time of the hope against hope. As it throb for the very next split second that will arise at the opening and closing of the eye. Every moment makes a difference when I'm near that desire that embraces an essence of your natural existence. Pausing in the mist of each knock at the door within the core of your spirit of, which is driven by faintly heard echoing beat. Saying it again can only place a dwelling hindrance upon the reenactment that must be identified amongst the two of us. Lead me not away from the tears of the source of pleasure, but of sorrow that is borrowed from dimness of a lost soul. Obstruction is not an end result in this occurrence, for it must maintain a stability to react to going on, as it was foreseen.

DAYSPRINGS

Followed, but led by the blind chirping birds of a high-pitched sound of misfortune. Soaring near to the ground with one-dimensional eye that looks upon thy. The darken skies of the moon cast a curse of dispirited abounding wings that are to be bounded by a willow tree. That of those shadows so as to depict the vastly way you are seen on those blossoming twigs. The sensation of perceiving light that of brightness. For which it will come into sight the first light of classical art. The frame is to be arranged or adjusted for this purpose to form silently with the beaks of the heartfelt manifestations. Forbid the mysterious haze to bring a day-to-day aspiration seen in your mind's eye to be brought a halt.

BEHOLD AS THE STORM DIMINISH

As the cold and warm front collide, causing a rival within a calm atmosphere. The sky has become sunless, as the winds increase. The weather siren is now warning those who are not prepared for a deceitful storm. A storm that has became odorless and tasteless. This impure storm is flooding the mortal environment that affects humanity. After a downpour of misleading speculation it has become a senseless storm. The sun has arisen to denounce the deceitful storm. Behold as the storm diminishes and the sky has become cloudless to create a brighter outlook. Seize this moment in a timeless atmosphere within a boundless environment to revel. For we shall not dwell upon foolishness, but upon the judiciousness of a human evolution.

VANISHING MIST

Be not afraid of that bring forward confusion. It is not what it seems to be. Seeing does not make believable, but feeling is of belief. Got day and night in reverse as you attempt to put into practice what you heard. First in last, but can't make out the mask that cover the face. Catch a glimpse of what is now there and gone away.

JUST LET US LIVE JUST A LITTLE WHILE LONGER

Every sunset we lie down to dwell upon tomorrow, which is not promise unto us. Let it be told for it's already sold unto those who are undeveloped, but not unto the profound. The spirits are beginning to distant themselves from the flesh to distinguish thy coolness from thy warmth. For our spirits does not belong to this clock that's ticking and tucking with a bird that's singing lullabies at the rising of the moon. Are we dooming as we presume the position that's stuck with the crack tone stones. We breathe, but without waiting for our pulse to react. Never the less our flesh is being traumatized by the lies that are folded away. Surrender the transgressions that are burdens unto the spirits, for tomorrow will be everlasting. Just let us live just a little while longer is already concluded within an empyrean, which the spirits await to raise again.

ENDURANCE OF A PENNILESS BEING

Digesting the mouth that hasn't been fed, as the tongue becomes a burning red. Walking towards that apple tree that seems to be vanishing as we prepare to bear fruit from its original evolution. Why is it every time we try to dry our face we cry with only one tear dropping from the eyes that reflects upon the abandoned? As the disposition beholds the fragile, but unmistakably divided, it's begun to unveil the true tale known to men. We continue to stress this line without placing that bottle of wine to our waterless lips. Tip the rounded, but hollow bowl that has no control over the blessings that overflows, as we grow. Say woe, as we go up and down on a roller coaster ride that moves along a high, sharply winding trestle with steep inclines. As that ride begins to slow we know that we're not going to blow the chance to enhance what's already in thy plans of he that stand over man. They say men are projected within the outlining of our souls. Now down below is hot not cold and there is no trace of endless struggles, because endurance of a penniless being lies upon the noble man timeless nourishing to what will not surrender to the physical desires.

WITHOUT I'M NOT

I journey with wounded heart plead brings forth my grief that is attempting to oppress their conviction. Marching as I face the trouble night of afflictions. Crying silently with no thought of letdowns. Fall to my kneels, but I get up and lift my hands to the heavens of one set of hands. Those unchanging hands that of which carries my yokes. Without I'm not as I travel with thy higher being.

STRENGTHENING A RESTRAINED WILL

A faint, but glaring light is shining within a shiftless sky flooded with a cloud of starved birds of a feather. Now weather they are located in the north or south are something those images knew nothing about. Shouted out are the silent words of the vanishing breeze within the funnel of vicious winds. A repetition of sound produced by the reflection of sound waves from a fractured covering has aroused. That of which was an unusual sound to very few, but was familiar to all that knew. That clue led them over a small pool of rainwater on the ground; this is watch over by a devout being who wear a crown. The clock was ticking as the flock of birds of a feather heard the words, come for I am here to wash away the evil that led you astray. For its said, if spiritually fed, strengthening a restrained will is to be continuously.

REPENTANCE WITH REMORSE

We begin by looking toward the deep seas that carries a large breeze of regrets along the shore. The sea then begins sending waving movements among the thoughts. The hole that we fear, that of which it can grab a hold of the weakness shown by the weeping willow. It whispers to you secretly regarding the guilt that has sat along the body of water that is revolving inward. The minds and souls are now suffocating by submerging in the body of water. The heart begin pumping poison that kills into the body of water that permit life. Repentance and remorse is something used to pull the mind and soul above the poison that causes corruption and death among us.

STRUGGLING TO KNOCK SOFTLY

As we pace the hollow floors of empty halls that are surround by the doors of limitations. It's difficult to be free when we're being held hostage by the walls of chains. Suddenly the rising of the sun overshadow the sleepless pace of overwhelming and painful thoughts. Thoughts of being weaken before facing the intangible barriers of misfortunes. A pounding noise has arouses to be heard, but it's very faint. As we search for that sound by placing our ears of thoughts upon the doors from which the pounding sounds of freedom has rattled the chains that hold us hostage. The thoughts of freedom will lead us not through temptations, but deliver us from the evildoers who trespass against us. The halls are filling with sounds that contain a degree of concentration. For hopelessness is now fulfilled with hopefulness that will cause the walls of chains to crumble and cause us to be free to knock softly.

BURNING TRAIL OF LIKELIHOOD

Passing through on those oppressive impose sanction that let not. It hasn't been unchallenging with no sudden tumble over the hollow sparks. Arousing to become aware of that broken rubbish. For it must be given a chance to bring to light its actual untreated self. Frightened I am of the shadowy ways you are visualized as. Taking the wind out of your open fire on an unpleasantly bitter hour of darkness. Shriving to tread that way of being on to the panting means of revise episodes. Get up and go to the approaching suffering to bring to an end. Pass through with dampness of ones piece of garment of closeness brings a sense of guidance contained by hope.

STROLLING UNDERNEATH

To walk back and forth with uneasiness about easily broken urgencies that has been abandon. Longing for that vital consequence that give rising to the window that allow a puff of air in good nature. Holds your tongue, for the cottonmouth awaits those droplets that are fill with tears. Clinching that vaguely thought that surround the tree of reasoning with self.

WHISPERING WITHOUT END

Hollow waterfalls filled with tears of repentance surround itself within water to create desirability. Let the spring water be absorbed by that oral cavity that's watertight with soft flowing streams. So as to be unclear, but cloudless droplet of something springs into being or from which it derives or is obtained. It too has a dwelling located above the core of an external passage leading to the hereafter.

THIS DAY

It seems to be far away, but yet some things are not set in stone without help. I'm nearer than yesterday therefore I won't fade away. Please stay as you are to reflect upon those whittle away for a bare cause. I wouldn't stray, for I will spray down your tomorrow for my amazement. That of which is already to be made use of. Tuck away this sorrowfulness for this day.

YESTERDAY SINS MEANS NOTHING COMPARED TO TODAY

Yesterday sins means nothing compared to Today
Yesterday sins means nothing compared to Today
Oh yesterday I was a sinner
Oh yesterday I was a sinner
See it was yesterday I did not know a common man that was spit on, talk about, and beat down to the fleshy tissue in which was to be cast off for you and I.
See it was yesterday I did not pick up the cross to follow that man that paid the price
Oh, Yesterday I knew not what it meant to know him
Oh, Yesterday I knew not what it meant to carry the cross
I was falling into that hole of no return until I saw a colorless hand with blood dipping.
I was lifted up and turn around, as feet were place on solid ground.

LEGENDS OF THEIR OWN TIME CAUSED BY THE DROUGHT

The journey traveled from one place to another by distance covered in a specified time. The desert has shined upon to be the destination of many men and women. As the sun begins to become dim by the hour, as the sand of time drift through the glass that is very fragile. The moisture within loses its retard. The soil is becoming dryer than usual. The soil is in need of a dam to encourage the moist to return to the foundation of the soil. The soil resist mode set in to overcome the dams', rejoin with the soil. The dam then begins to calmly place itself in a position that revolves around a difficult task thrown before it. The dam is now offering its proposal to the hollow underground by asking it to regress. The dam is now recognized as one of the soldiers of the senior dam. The Saints of the soil then begin joining in to resolve this matter or matters. It sometime ended within a war or in a peaceful and nonviolent fashion in the eyes of history. The dam is now the legend of that time caused by the drought.

THE VALLEY OF

HOLLOW FOOTSTEPS

Journey into the past that has a pair of empty shoes that must be filled. The emptiness is face to face with an extensive area of land drained by a feeling of being heavily burden. A forbidden sound created by an echo has surface to invade the footsteps of the unjust. The act of terror has transformed the vital signs' that's influencing the conditions, which threaten the thoughtless reflection. Cast away the similarities that focus on the battleground stumble upon. Reactivate the stump that causes the circulation to flow throw the valley of prosperity. Let it be known that the footsteps will not be made alone. For those who choose a hollow path shall loose its meaning and become empty.

RISING ABOVE THE GHETTO PAIN

As the early morning hour approaches and the sun rises in the mist of the sky. Awaking to watch the brand new day blossom as if it was a flower on a bright spring day. The birds are whistling as the subway train passes through the city causing the windows to tremble, as if a band was playing a melody tone pleasing to the ear. The shower water is running as I stand up under it and think of the hostile ways that embrace itself around humanity. As I walk through a house torn by the torment that is extremely painful As I focus on the reflection of the windstorm of great violence among the mourn within the streets Although mountains are not high enough and the trees' are not tall enough to hold me down under the rug of disqualification. As the clouds of pollution, causes rain to pour into my thoughts. I am rising with the clouds of freedom from all extraneous ghetto matters that will become painless to those that expect to exhale every morning.

THE PAIN AND PRAYERS OF THE YOUNG SOULS

Our father it's hard for us to swallow what's known to be sour. Young ones are being devoured by the hour. Which art in heaven we either hit seven or eleven or blow out. Hallowed be thy name, for it's hard to explain the pains of our young hearts, because of change. Thy kingdom comes, for thy spirits are numb. Thy will be done as one in earth, caused by the thirst that await the fountain of many verses of the bible for survival. For what we are told that it is in heaven. Give us this day, for we're not dead, as receive our daily bread. Forgive us of our debts, as you save us from ourselves. For we forgive our debtors that mean us no harm. Lead we not into temptation, as our revelation slowly come to pass over. Deliver us from evil, therefore we shall not see nor hear. For thine is the kingdom for which we stand to rejoice unto our savior. For the power that which uplifts the young minds, hearts, and souls. For the glory that which is yours forever. Amen

THE YOUNG LOST SPIRITS OF THE UNIVERSE

As the small stars lie their lives down in the mist of the frontier of the unfound galaxy, cause they have no where to shine. As they drift into an unsettled and uncultivated region left in its natural condition, as if it has to abstain gravity They live among a solar system that is lacking sympathy, feelings, nor concern. It is a struggle that prohibits them to be able to escape from those conditions. They are lost and in need of assistance to search for their soul purpose. Sometimes they are left wondering off into space thinking with the absence of sound What will bring about tomorrow sometimes floats into the empty spaces within the minds of the stars? The spirits have now entered the dark and barricade solar eclipse that hides' the bright side of the stars, because the solar system is full of betrayal. The first step made, as a cavity of vehemence was let down upon. The hearts of the stars begins throbbing, as they leak forming a chemical element of corruption. The chemical element is leaving a trail of criticism that leaks into a gray area of hopelessness. It then begins to uncover the emotional and spiritual breeze that stands still between the greatest conception of the past, present, and future Their guards are beginning to fall, as if the reflection of time is merging to cause an explosion of meaningless death among the galaxies. That of many ordeals allows the galaxies to take captive of the choices that will capture a decisive moment or dare to shine among one another.

THE TRIALS AND TRIBULATIONS OF THE YOUNG SHADOWS

The shadows are losing their strength that's projected by the rays of the flames. The flames are getting smaller and the water is beginning to wash away the dreams and goals of our shadows. It seems to them that the wood is turning into ashes that will blow away in the wind. As it become invisible to the eyes that reflects the vision to over come the lost. The shadows legs are weakling as they shake and tremble from the fear of being an endanger species. The knees of the shadows are now touching the bottom of the well of prayers. As they float away slowly down the river where judgment takes place. As the smoke of the flames that are half way burned out rises, it's being inhaled by the shadows that have inherited the vital forces of the immortal parts of their souls. The frames of the shadows are suffering and becoming wasted as it enters the twilight zone. The eclipse is now covering the light that stimulates a positive visual perception of the flames. The flames must rejuvenate in order to resurrect the positive of the shadows that surrounds the world.

MY GENERATION IS SLOWLY FADING AWAY

As my generation slowly fades away day by day crumbling into small pieces, as we think how the world really is. There's a large number of painful deaths and very little painless deaths. Sometimes my generation says to themselves there's no place like the home that is up above so, so, far away. There comes a time in every person life where their heart fades off into the dark ways of life. My generation thought that their time would never come, but the candle light is slowly burning away. We feel as if the whole world is against us, but we're wrong. We do feel like our judgment day is drawing near although there is no fear, because death to us is like falling into a deeper and darker hole. As we walk alone in the valley of darkness, we think of the dreams we had on the bright side of life, but when we re-enter this world we will fulfill our dreams.

Have merciful thoughts upon us for we mean no harm upon you,

LET NOT YOUR MIND BE TROUBLE

Let not your divine mind be trouble, for those who don't will want for more. Examine the sunshine and don't expect to inspect the clouds. Be very proud as a child and let not your conception race ferociously. Temptation will trail you throughout your being and won't be anything pleasing. Believe and you will receive the knowledge to trace your place in this race we are running. Watch ahead for you're alive and not dead. Spread the word and confess to other about the bread you've consumed. Capture a potion out of the fountain that will convert you to desire an answer to all your dilemmas. Letting your mind not be trouble will help resolve them as a whole.

FOR IT'S SOUR
TASTING OR NOT

Oppressing the culture and tongue of the brown skin, for its sour tasting. Separating families from one another, for its sour tasting.

Escaping within the Underground Railroad to seek freedom, for its not sour tasting.

Institutionalizing the minds of the free man to cause low functioning, for its sour tasting.

Watching ancestors hanging from the tree is terrifying, for it's sour tasting.

Those who committed crimes of that nature are being processed in the court of law, for its not sour tasting.

From within the past to the future we've got here, watching over our shoulder wandering if we would be shot in the back, for its sour tasting.

Where will the next meal arouse from, as we sit silently to count the breadcrumbs, for its sour tasting?

The long and struggling days or night we absorb the rain droplets that allow us to feed our hungry branches, for it's sour tasting or not.

Those corners on a full moon night seem to create a fog with a howl from an unusual dog, for its sour tasting.

Those who are clueless of the consequence are unveiling drug deals, for its sour tasting.

Streetlights are blowing out as the storm arises to sweep away sinful ways, for its sour tasting.

Another bullet has enter the body, as it pears the soul when exiting, for its sour tasting.

We will make our way passed that wound to rising as the moon set, for its not sour tasting.

We should close this chapter of this book to move forward with peace amongst all, for its not sour tasting.

UNWAVERING

I'm trying to hold on to the unchanging hand that stretches out. I'm blind in hope to see one day. I have a broken heart that's beating faintly. My legs are giving out. It's difficult to do so as the clouds hover over my head. My spirit is yet strong as everything goes wrong. This journey seems to be long suffering as I am fighting for breath. I hold my head up with tears of faith as I look to the hills in which all my help comes from. I've been rescue from harm, danger or loss as the consequences of sin has been redeemed.

UNDERGROUND RAILROAD OF MIRACULOUS SOULS

As the night approaches and the moon arise to pour forth the radiance for the struggle to see with the spiritual eyes. A prolonged, but mournful cry to be liberated has echo in the naked ears of many that are held in captivity. As the spiritual feet breed to leave a trail that will lead many souls to the beginning and not the end. Thee hum to cast a blameless sound which cometh forth to the calling of the defenseless ghosts of enslavement. They're traveling through the fields that are being used to suppress those who will awake to a chilling night. After the heated day and dogs, that tracks the odor that aroused from aged ancestry. Don't stop strengthening the intention, for it's to follow the footsteps that were made within the underground railroad that have freed many miraculous souls.

DEEPLY ROOTED

Something that serves as the means to attach to the soil of that which I is. I absorb the draining water that come from the clouds of reason. Each climate changes within different spells. Some are colder than other and that of which I derived from is drawing me nearer. Despite the fact the lukewarm bring about evolution within me. A star that is basis of the solar system and sustains life is shining brightly upon me as I steadfast to receive one of my many types of nourishment. Having established an indigenous relationship with my environment, I continue to exist.

MOTHER MAY I

Mother may I awaken to take your hand as we both approach this journey toward a timeless existence.

Mother may I emphasize the impact of your unconditional devotion for your child.

Mother may I smile to reflect the joyous feeling I receive every time your likeness emerges.

Mother may I pour forth these teardrops that are yearning deep within the midst of my heart in fear of missing that attachment as I mature.

Mother may I look upon the fullness of everyday with you, for they are treasured.

Mother may I come to see that miraculous garden of green pasture, which leads us not into darkness that's reflecting little or no light to witness the renowned willingness to survive.

Mother may I only ask of you to arise as I return all that was given to I as a gift from within your beautiful soul.

"Love always your child"

UNBORN CHILD

A feeling of a heart beating within a womb is there. A part of my being and someone else is floating in the bounds of me. I shed tears of joy down my face to reveal indebtedness. A life within a living essence will develop as I anticipate the arrival. A sensation contained by numbness is rumbling deeply within. I try to image the outer shell that will impose it's thank giving as it come to take it first breath.

AFTER THE WHILE MY CHILD

As leading lights descend out of the vault of heaven, I kneel to reveal the real explanation you're here at this time. Sit near as the thirstiness zoom in on the first tear droplet of understanding that fell from the sky. I must not tilt the true as I see that earliest tooth of curiosity. Look up as I tuck you in, for the story never ends. The wise tell started in the garden that was hardened by that bit into the forbidden fruit of judgment. That of which causes us to smile and frown due to those ups and downs. Yet you were born with that crown that made you my prince or princess that will shine after while my child.

YOUNG WEEPING LEAVES OF COLOR

Not long ago it was promising and the trees were noble without a single obscure hanging over. The trees tell a fictitious story on vigorous experiences, as confusion and frustration set within the young leaves method of reflecting. Take not the umbrella of honor that which was given unto the leaves as a shield. As a transition takes place the unfriendliness is causing a passionless breeze to be unleashed. The branches are being restrained by the dreadful action that lies within the trees. The trees are reaping what they've sowed as the leaves are struggling not to be separated from the branches of life. Come and let us make a humble entreaty until the trees of many unknown transgressions are surrender unto thy one of relentless mercy. A demonstration of repentance must arouse to enhance the warmth of the branches that are attached to the leaves. Put forth the warmth that will lay down a foundation for those that will have merciful value on life continuance. For the weeping leaves will laugh with unique colors of a believable future.

YEARNING DEEPLY FOR

As I close my eyes to enter a dimension that creates a priceless internal and external lining of your comeliness. Your spiritual being has put forth a strong attractive charm with a warm unseen affection. This is drawing me to those eyes that have an unforgettable likeness of the rising of the sun. A steady force, as the wind propels the hair that embraces your untainted mind of divine thoughts, which abounds from those slightly damp lips. Capturing that sweet, viscid fluid produced by me from the nectar collected from your expression that I must preserve. I tilt the upper part of my physical existence, for I see this as an elegant task that must be attain with relentless loyalty. Those concealed but visible midpoint within a shelter fill with that sinless lineage, this I am yearning deeply for.

TO MY LOVE

Once a upon a time

My Love in which I have a weakness for.

My Love you're the first light that my sight long for each morning as I'm yearning for you.

My Love causes me to kiss and hug you early in the day before I go away.

My Love every heart beat is strong when I'm home and becomes weak when I'm gone.

My Love let me take you by the hand and spread it over that romance you so desire until we breathe our last

In Love
Undyingly & Everlastingly

FLOWERS CREATE BEAUTIFUL FAITH

Seasons are changing to create a particular condition within an ageless garden. A chilly breeze has surface to cause a transition that will transpire a disturbance. Confusion set apace of-which is created by winds of many dissimilar air masses. The buds of many flowers are being heavily weigh down by the frost that upon them. The buds freeze and begin to break from the stems leaving them breathless. As the flowers await the coming of the season that will simulate the blossoms of new lives. A mass of warm air has emerged to nurture a formula of words used in praying. A slight manifestation has aroused to create a ray of hope. The ray that shine the light upon the stems, causing the buds to be born again. For life is given to those who allow a miraculous offspring to occur within the garden. Let flowers blossom to create beautiful faith amongst us.

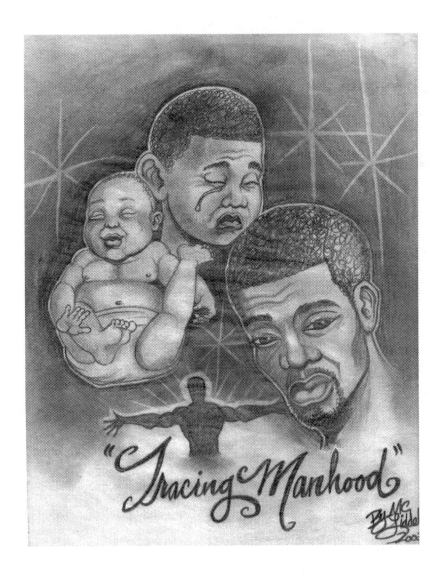

TRACING MANHOOD

Traveling back might seem to far, but this is how we find out who we are. As a child we're told to wait a while. For what you'll become will make you proud? As we roar like thunder it makes us wonder. Now take it in consideration that we're part of a generation that embrace society with love and hate. Masculine is what we are, but frequently we're easily hurt by the dirt from which we were created. Don't take that for granted for we're human with many heroic qualities. Whispering is likely to be the sound of an adolescent trying to declare truth or dare. For the badge of courage is now worn to signalize having attained maturity. Silence arouses as the strength increase to transpire a transformation.

SEEK OUT

He look upon that of are my eyes that are of my reflection. I try, but miss the cause of my vision. The ears hear what is in secret. Hidden is the tongue of many word of distinctiveness. The lips are of dryness from the forced wind and unheard sounds. Saying nothing leads to the nonexistent, but speaks high volume within self.

EXISTING

Is it our reflections that look upon us as we look intently at the livelihood of identity? That face alive with mischief with out the moral coating. From birth, we have that sensation of the dryness in the mouth and throat, which is the need or desire for knowledge. We give the impression of a nothingness curse that seems to direct to or toward itself or oneself. For that is the act or process judging the formation of opinion after consideration or deliberation? The unfinished extraction of life has penetrated the body of water, which encourage us to participate in the coming influential habits. Having asked, knocks, and seeks at the door, which possess the treasures of wisdom that will replenish the abandoned within the unexpressive existence. We are here with a thin coating of mortality, for we must not become quenched, but worthy of the lastingness.

LOST, BUT FOUND

Where am I, comes to the minds of many who don't know. Come let us walk freely without tripping over what is not there. Sharing the space that's already shaded in by the mass that which is measureless. Now that we have found the grounds for which we stand on, being lost has come to past.

SURVIVING PIECES

Day of old is bewildered by that of which is nameless. Carelessly moving and disarranging things that show all the dismissive gesture. Features becomes manifest, but gives up a faint "polished surface twinned face and chest in reverse". A slanted shadow will not hold the physical structure of matter that forms a whole but has no definable shape. The utterance of grief or sorrow who is fumbling for words forced from a tightlipped ness. The discomfort, weakness, or pain caused by a prolonged lack of rightness. Free of the knees, and in the legs, with a sore botch that cannot be healed, from the sole of thy foot.

THE RESTLESSNESS OF THE WIND

As the wind lie awake unable to relax, causing a breeze to sweep inward with a distinctive sound. It leaves itself airless with the absence of sound. Corruption is now trying to set its course to cause confusion. Its purpose is to leave the wind motionless. For what's invisible must have movement to indicate what direction it's headed. An environment naturally suited is now lacking an element that helps create immortality amongst all. The wind shifts, as it blows outward creating an unexpected attack on the meaningless deaths. The emptiness now being filled with spiritual sounds of the wind. Come let us forgive the corrupted, for thy forgiveness of a higher power is granted to all that allow it to. Now thy restless wind can rest within life itself.

ROARING MERCIFULLY UPON THE SLEEPING

The young lions roared, as if they where trying to bring forth fears which echo's near the many ears of the wilderness. The fountain of living water stood still, for it was mistakenly preyed upon. Therefore the showers have been withholding and there has been no latter rain for those who refuse to be ashamed. The trees whispered softly, but could be blame, for the breeze was at ease, as for the wild that used the wilderness to snuff up the wind. Those thieves of the darkness are on the prowl once again to try to bend the truth about no end. Wherefore, mountains of many faces will the sheep's prevail from the trouble thieves of no beliefs. In vain the echo smitten the sheep's; they received no guilders: the fearless have devoured the foolish, like destroying lions. Lead us not through the wilderness, through the land of deserts, pits, and of the shadows of faint vision. This land is where no man should have to pass through and where no man should dwelt. Let the hungry be fed, for the curse shall be lifted. The living water shall quench the thirst of the flesh, for it shall not want. Trees shall breath freely as the roots roar mercifully upon those who were sleeping silently to echo awareness of the coming.

RISING ABOVE THE BLACK AND WHITE SMOKE

Once a point of time there was no such thing as color. There was not a different in our beliefs: full acceptance of a thing as it truly is. Sometimes we'll all find ourselves blinded by the smoke that rises from the frames of hate. We then began choking and the compression of the wind begins to slow down leaving us breathless. The birds then begin whistling the sound made by forcing breath through rounded and nearly closed lips of hope. The tears are dripping from the clouds of lonely eyes that are blinded by hate among one another. Nourishing the frames of hate by feeding into the separation of colors. Flowers are red and sometimes blue, but that don't hide the inherent quality in an object of pleasing the eye. Reaching for the sky that which is full of color in the day and the night brings on the black sky and the white bright stars of hope that rises above the smoke that is full of hate.

AS NOT FOR TWO, BUT
AS FOR ONE

In the beginning the more I called upon you the more you rebelled, causing us to see only a duplicate. I never stopped offering your eternal eyes the sacrifices within myself. I knew there was a time I took you by the arm only to ask you to walk with me to speak of the silent past, for you would not admit that I was the one who healed a fragment of your heart. I led you to me with kindness and with love, not with a rope. I held you close to me; I bent down to feed our soul, but it was not I you trusted, instead you allow the deceitfulness of the present to guide your mind and body elsewhere. I will roar like a lion, for you will return trembling from the thought of the chilling breeze that escaped my slightly open soul that had once swept you off your feet. You'll see, for you will come back fluttering like a bird from the north as the season reflect the true image within those everlasting eyes that lies upon your beautiful face. It will be then I will bring you back across the thin line between that intense affectionate or passionate attraction we have for one another.

FACE TO FACE

Gazing within the untaken eyes of my inner faith, caused by throbbing time pieces of survival. For a reflection of nature has transform into a root attached to I am. This of which is a mouth full of air that trying to come to terms with my disobedience. The body lies stiff while the deeply-rooted revive the moral fiber. Revival will transpire throw away of fine-tuning. Stop hiding from the inner shell that nurtures the outer shell of anticipation.

ESCAPING THE VESSEL OF CAPTIVITY

The reflection of a crest vessel has arisen to recreate the massacre of many spirits. The vessel roam upon the Black Sea, as the souls and minds are being silent to await trial. We have floated upon the beginning of a passage that's unearthly. Those who reach out will witness a profound silence within. For it's forbidden not to exhilarate one another, because those who don't will vanish. A stench has aroused from the lifeless spirits that lie amongst the living, causing manifestation to rise with mournful sounds. A sacrifice of a physical mass must take place to awaken the suffering of others. A worthy force is driving out the torment. As the light seep through a cavity in the vessel allowing the spirits to distinguish where they're heading. The vessel of captivity is approaching the soil that creates liberty amongst all. Free will is expressed within when given a chance to place our feet deep within the soil to absorb freedom.

CRUMBLING SHACKLES

Let me go has been the echo of the rattling restraints. This can not be you see. I am supposed to be without metal fastening for encircling and confining to thy ankles and wrists. Tripping over oppression as I fall, but I get up to walk towards the burning light to obtain the same as it should be for every one of us who want. Pieces the shackles are crumbling as I stagger with regard to my hand and feet being boundless.

NOT GUILTY OF

Not guilty of having the characteristic within the limits of human capabilities.

Not guilty of having faith in my beliefs.

Not guilty of a painful loss of pride or self-respect.

Not guilty of being fruitful within a restricted environment.

Not guilty of the knowledge, understanding, and wisdom I absorbed from a divine being.

Not guilty of a repetition of a sound produced by the reflection of the freedom from captivity or confinement of ones physical being.

Not guilty of an unlawful thing of nature, which is harmful to others?

Not guilty of a fragment of the American dream.

Not guilty of loving thy neighbor, nevertheless hating them.

Not guilty of enhancing the foundation, which has been built for my family.

Not guilty of the testimony I have given unto those who will listen

UNBOUNDED CONVICTION

Hold thy right hand upon the heart of many throbs to do better. Tell to those that know not to be of nobility without any fear of man. Fly free, as if you were a bird of many wings. That of which you carry will carry in return. Stand firm on the street of prospects. Imperfect cannot be of doubt, but trust among character.

REVITALIZING A
BOUNDLESS PASSAGE

The grounds for which we have stood on with our barefoot have begun to shake involuntarily, as from fear. It has become obvious that the grounds are being separated by the fatalities. A dose of formality has been stripped from our thoughts leaving us barefaced, but not unmindful. Drowsiness is trying to creep within the naked eyes, but is awaken by thunderous sounds of weeping drums. A voyage has been walk upon and a pounding noise causes it to become disengaged. As we begin to move on foot at a moderate pace a mirage appears to be gazing within our noble eyes. The image of ourselves, that which is reflecting a revitalization of the boundless being. It's to originate the right or freedom to pass through to the situated in corresponding positions across an intervening line.

BREATHING UNCONSCIOUSLY

I stagger as my pulse drums at a restrained pace within. I function as my anxiety scramble involuntarily. My habitat portrayal extracts its submissive existence without means of. I embark on the airless passageway unwittingly as the windowpane is converted into disbelief. Panic not as I drift into an unchanged sketch that gives the impression of being purposelessness. Breaking free from the dissolution of self to encounter the undreamed of, but within reach of my mind's eye.

THUS COME TO PASS

You're carried along by the currents of air and water beyond the shoreline. Taken away from what you thought you had a handle on, but flooded with nothing. Rushed off your feet to witness what is not. Sandy dust causes blurriness before now over the balanced eyes. Impulses come into the way of undertaking an impassiveness trail of no end. It's pour out the boundary of your thoughts that signal, stimulating the amount of electric charges flowing past a specified pathway at a defining moment. The emotion erupts with lukewarm faith in the yet to come change or transformation.

WILLING TREE

The out of order world was unlocked and a small seed of faith descent into the hairline fracture of the earth core. That seed was nurture with anticipation of what was to come to pass. The sun shined with just a crack of dawn, as the silence led the unsighted by means of endurance and purpose. The break free of the tree was effortlessness, because they knew not. The spring had been converted into a waterless and thirsty inner self due to the lack of wholeheartedness. The carving of the tree shapes the battleground for the living wage. To the forefront comes deliverance, but not an ordinary will. Lying down and stretching out the arms of existence by means of the departure of death.

Two hands were nailed upon me

Two nails were place in the waist and me

Two feet were nailed upon me

The blood covered the tree causing it to fade behind the shadow of the son. The crowned head hung down, as the tree embrace to fulfill merciful and gracious command.

BOWING HEADS

Step forward to discover what is to be. Those of what line will you and I draw before we surrender unto he that serve the wrongdoers. Reveal that of which is heavy on the heart. Come let you and I bend our heads and knee to plead our set of conditions that has been laid before us. The up right post with a transverse piece upon it, in which he was crucified, has set eyes on you and me. He's staring without sound upon our end and beginning waiting with patience. Turn willingly as face the truth that will delivery us to and from the troubles that of the past and present.

SINCERELY HUNGERING FOR THE TRUTH

Hungering for the truth is beyond our pond of life. We must free our intentions and become immortal to this dimension. Gaining the truth to us is unusually challenging. That's why it's so breathtaking. Creating change is the first measure to lore the truth. We must become strong to carry on. Even though we're at our uppermost and sometimes at our downfall. We also feel like there is no one around to acknowledge the pain of all humankind. Some humans in this timeless dimension feel that actuality is injustice, but others say that it makes them feel adequate. So should we always sing a song, as if others are wrong? As we all moan, as if the truth is postponed. We have suspicion, but don't sometime live long enough to lore our mission. The truth shall set us free from all evil and that should be worthy enough for you and me.

FINISHING THE EVENING MEAL

A period that fast approaches us with decreasing daylight between dawn and dust. Those who are seated shall take part. Take this bread that contains words, for it will be digested to fill nothingness. These crumbs will penetrate the moral fiber to convey the purpose. Get a hold of the cup that you will sip slowly from to quench your need for solutions. For who that wait for that sweet course or dish that will be served at the end of this extensive feast will dwell evermore.

AWAKEN TO SEE AND HEAR
THE DIVINENESS OF DIVERSITY

As thunder begins rumbling as if it's to declaim or rage with loud voices. A revival of interest or conscience that will overcome the emptiness of the hollow hearts. As the sun rises and set its reflection upon the eyes of many souls causing them to blossom with colorful similarities. The moon begins to await its moment to shine upon the shadows of humanity. To be or not to be free of different cultures, abilities, religions, sexes, and races of equally valuable members of our society. Time is becoming the anchor of a heavy stone of grief. We must provide the stone with insufficient nourishment by refusing to claim or accept put down of others. Depriving and the disperse of many must go up in smoke, as if it's the ghost of our time. The false image, often faint with the resemblance of a misfortune of many generations. Revealing the truth will give us pride in our human nature. The spiritual eyes project a positive description of mankind. The spiritual ears retrieve the wisdom and knowledge to perceive the challenges that are ahead. The spiritual hearts echoes with harmony, which bring peace and friendliness among races.

WIDE AWAKE

Having my eyes cover for so long has allowed me to be prepared to listen for the sound that's procrastinating, causing the movement to slow. For that reason several visions has appeared within the darkness, which has portrayed the weakness amongst the living and the strength that surrounds the dead. Not he that arouses from sleeps; wake up. This cloth case stuffed with feathers used to cushion the head to keep me snoozing is quietly slipping away. Lying down has surrendered and escaped the chain of thought. Breaking away from a fold of skin that closes over those eyes and letting the light shine within a nondescript insight. Looking upon those who exhibit a strong desire, as for high achievement.

BLACK, BUT SHADED IN WITH BROWN

It's you and I, but we both fail shy of the dirty covering that we are known to be. You see that of what you have labeled me to be, yes the color of what is reflected up under a shady tree or that shadow that follows me throughout my being. Oh, try to roam with a black cloud hovered over your head that does nothing but releases a downpour of dishonorable reflections upon you. As I examining my demeanor and my identity, it has come before me that of what's projected through the eyes of my descend was the layout of the time that is to come hereafter. I'm not that black bloodthirsty whip that victimized and deprived the way of living built for the means of survival. The darkness that lies beneath that sunless upper atmosphere within the earth, that's not I. As for those stainless steel barricades that are holding innocent brown faces in bondage to cast off the natural covering. When it's all reveal the chains would crumble, as the scab forms over a healing wound to create a noble being. For I smile without a frown, because I'm black, but shaded in with brown.

YOU AND I SHALL

You and I shall awaken to see the world, which we live in with one another.

You and I shall live as neighbors with one another, for there is no color.

You and I shall pastime with one another as each day arises.

You and I shall sit and have supper with one another, for it will fill our souls.

You and I shall develop without hate, but with love for one another.

You and I shall encourage one another to demolish the barrier that hinders our progress.

You and I shall terminate the violence or sob with one another.

You and I shall not fear one another, for he's near.

You and I shall be joyous and not jealous of one another.

You and I shall witness the glorious days that lie ahead with one another, for they're not gray.

You and I shall seek a passage that will steer us to the streets of prosperity, for we're unearthly sisters or brothers.

You and I shall have a testimony relating to the coming and exiting of each life that shines with a divine gloss, for that will not be lost.

A FRAGMENT OF THE BROKEN PUZZLE

A box is open, but too many pieces seem to be missing. Although we begin to try to assemble what is not, therefore you have disregarded me to long. A box left open to wear and tear loses its image. It's to be search for with remorse, so why then my fair one have you forsaken me. Is boxes content no longer intriguing to the eyes and hands, which once they set aglow? Tried so hard to fit the opposite pieces within a deep pour that drives us into a comer. So your promises to mold me no matter how long it was just a promise. Wait not on the promises that are deceitful for it will create a dimmer light. I am still that colorful picture that you beg for and I might not have my gleam. For if you look deep in the center you can remember why you beg for me in the first place. Let me know what I am missing for I will seek it with hope of finding it. Close your eyes and remember when you took me off the shelf if you love me, then can't you love me now. For this must be the reason I sleep with one eye open to prevent the unthinkable. Well open them both and use the love you once had for me. Create in me what you saw so long ago for I have never needed your touch so much. For you are my knight and I am your princess, rescue me fair one. My heart and soul has been missing pieces to this puzzle all along, so come and we shall unite.

LINING UP

As we walk amongst our friends in the hall of many walls that were built
   for a cause.
We all sometime fall, but it is only for us to get back up.
Now we sit to drink from the cup of knowledge that fills our minds.
For it is time to take a look at the book that holds our future.
Stand up tall as you strive with pride in the line of those who tried.

WAY OUT, OF NO MEANS

She stares off into the skyline, as the radiance of the stars and moon reflect upon the river. The journey across the linkage to the other side while in deep-thought. Listening to those far away understanding. A different direction became grasping as she seeks the unchanged destination. Wondering how she made it to what she set sights on, not knowing that he carried her over. Memories lost in the wind, nevertheless delighted to be an element for this purpose. Accepted wisdom from the good and not the evil, for it comforts her.

UNDYING GARDEN

Come in the bounds of what
is recognize as the starting
point.
The forthcoming souls are
transplant in the clay of
being.
A mouthful of air was
exhale, a life emerge in the
image of itself.
As you struggle for breathe
to set eye on an incredible
sight for the naked eye
take heed to the tree of
knowledge that bares the
forbidden fruit.
Why or why not bit that of a
nature herein evil. Thoughts
will pour in into an
untainted way of thinking.
It whispers into those sinless
ears, do as I say, not as I do
was said.

Fall short of the long
awaited cure, which will
come forth as a sacrificial
lamb.
That of which, pleaded on
Mount Olive for our
wrongdoing, as for
justification.

STARVED BIRDS OF A QUILL

Surrounded by an
unguarded be winded
motionless picture, which is
of a weightless way of being.
Uninviting conditions are
inside of the frame of mind
that carries it away in
blustery weather.
Struggling to stay a flow,
as bits and pieces of
feathers of a malnourish
feathered vertebrates with
forelimbs modified to form
wings.
Keep in good condition with
constant and warmhearted
temperature of self-
determining environmental
warmth.

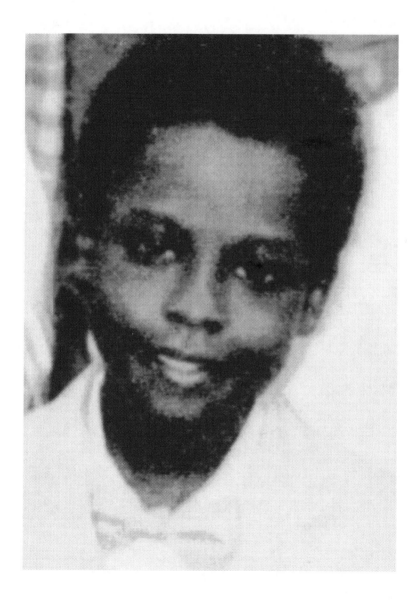

LAMARK

He is the driven force of
thy strength therein.
I am walking with Him on
a path of green grazing
land.
He guides thy alongside an
unruffled watercourse.
He steer thy down the true
passageway,
bringing nobility to his
identity.
Even as thy walk from
beginning to end of the
evil valley of loss of life.
"Thy shall not be troubled,
for he is nearby thy.

LET THAT OF IN

Life forms, take the weight
off your feet only to utter
words of serenity,
as you lay down your
arms.
It is okay to be of a genial
moral fiber,
rather than to be of
viciousness. Trickling off
the face of dimness are
droplets of feeling shame
of the closing stages.
Why are you locking in the
masses of trials and
breakdowns?
Let somebody in on the
facts of lose sleep,
as you let that of in to walk
off with those yokes.